DRAW WITH MOM

Two-Person Doodle Book

Lara Lang

© Copyright 2023 - All rights reserved.

You may not reproduce, duplicate or send the contents of this book without direct written permission from the author.

CHILD: Draw one thing you would pack for an adventure! Draw what you're wearing for this adventure!

CHILD

MOM: Draw another thing you'll need there! Add any animal companions you might bring along.

MOM

CHILD: Draw your favorite meal!

CHILD

MOM: Add your child's favorite snack and some details to the drawing (plates, cups, napkins, and so on)

MOM

CHILD: Invent an insect!

CHILD

MOM: Add elements to make it funny! (like a unibrow, a mustache, a silly or surprised expression)

MOM

CHILD: Draw your favorite vehicle!

CHILD

MOM: Add your least favorite vehicle to the drawing!

MOM

CHILD: Combine animals to create a new creature! Draw the head and the body!

CHILD

MOM: Add a tail and a new pair of ears!

MOM

CHILD: Start the drawing with a pair of eyes.

CHILD

MOM: Add an element to the drawing. Take turns adding elements back and forth.

MOM

CHILD: Draw a sky full of air balloons.

CHILD

MOM: What does each carry?

CHILD: Draw a tree with big branches!

CHILD

MOM: The tree bears something unexpected. What?

CHILD: Draw a home in outer space!

CHILD

MOM: Who lives there?

CHILD: Draw the biggest birthday cake you can imagine!

CHILD

MOM: Decorate it with your child's favorite candies!

MOM

CHILD: Fill the page with things with wheels!

CHILD

MOM: Fill the page with things that float!

MOM

CHILD: Make a drawing just with dots!

CHILD

MOM: Connect the dots and discover the image!

MOM

CHILD: Draw something you're afraid of! Give the object of your fear silly accessories, like a tutu, a hat, or a pair of sunglasses.

CHILD

MOM: Draw something you're afraid of! Make it play a game of chess or do a magic trick.

MOM

CHILD: Draw something that makes you happy!

CHILD

MOM: Draw something that makes you happy!

MOM

CHILD: Draw Mom as a superhero!

CHILD

MOM: Draw your kid as a superhero!

MOM

CHILD: Draw a weird costume!

CHILD

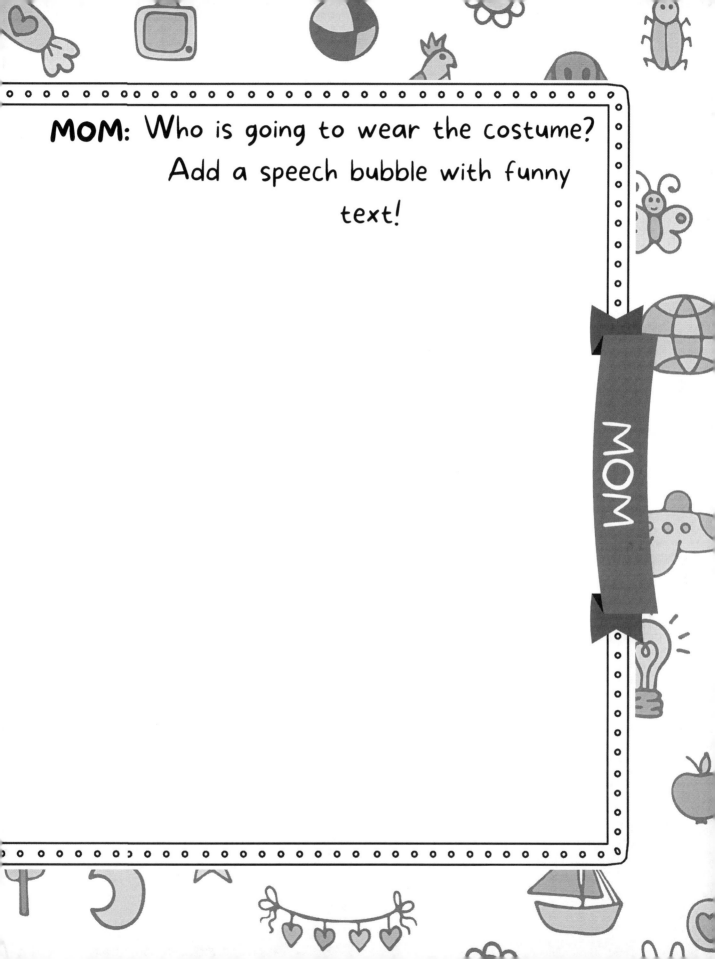

MOM: Who is going to wear the costume? Add a speech bubble with funny text!

MOM

CHILD: Draw the sky with the biggest rainbow you can imagine!

CHILD

MOM: Draw an unusual treasure at the end of the rainbow!

MOM

CHILD: Draw your favorite season!

CHILD

MOM: Draw your child's favorite activity in that season!

MOM

CHILD: Draw an object you can see right now!

CHILD

MOM: Draw the object you see in an absurd situation. (like a chair floating in mid-air or a lamp post sprouting legs and walking away).

MOM

CHILD: Draw a prehistoric land creature!

CHILD

MOM: Draw a prehistoric water creature!

MOM

CHILD: Draw 3 things that start with the letter "A"!

CHILD

MOM: Draw 3 things that start with the letter "C"!

MOM

CHILD: Draw smiley faces with different expressions!

CHILD

MOM: Guess what is the emotion for each one! Add different hairstyles for each smiley face!

MOM

CHILD: Draw a fruit sliced open!

MOM: Imagine a dessert made from the fruit, that your child would like. Draw it!

MOM

CHILD: Start the drawing with the outline of a house.

CHILD

MOM: Add an element to the drawing. Take turns adding elements back and forth.

MOM

CHILD: Draw your favorite cartoon character!

CHILD

MOM: Draw your favorite cartoon character from your childhood!

MOM

CHILD: Close your eyes and draw a quick scribble.

CHILD

MOM: Use the scribble as the starting point for your drawing.

MOM

CHILD: Draw something and then verbally explain to your Mom exactly how to draw what you have drawn.

MOM: Is there any resemblance to your child's drawing?

MOM

CHILD: Draw a treasure map.

CHILD

MOM: What does the treasure look like? Draw it!

MOM

CHILD: Draw an animal with superhero abilities!

MOM: What does his assistant look like?

CHILD: Draw 5 dots!

CHILD

MOM: Using those dots, draw a person.

MOM

CHILD: Draw yourself!

CHILD

MOM: Draw yourself!

CHILD: Draw your favorite toy!

CHILD

MOM: Draw your favorite toy from your childhood!

MOM

CHILD: Draw a big ship!

CHILD

MOM: Draw the captain on that ship! Add details to the environment!

CHILD: Draw Santa Claus with his big bag!!

CHILD

MOM: Add details to Santa's bag, and draw his favorite reindeer!

MOM

CHILD: Draw a cute cat with a big bow!

CHILD

MOM: Draw her twin sister!

MOM

CHILD: Start the drawing with a circle.

CHILD

MOM: Add an element to the drawing. Take turns adding elements back and forth.

MOM

CHILD: Start the drawing with a line!

CHILD

MOM: Add an element to the drawing. Take turns adding elements back and forth.

MOM

CHILD: Draw your favorite summer activity!

CHILD

MOM: Add elements to the background to make it more fun!

MOM

CHILD: If you were an animal, what would it be? Draw it!

CHILD

MOM: Where does it live? Draw the animal's home!

MOM

CHILD: Draw your name in fancy letters!

CHILD

MOM: Draw your name with the same character style!

CHILD: Draw yourself ten years in the future!

MOM: Draw yourself at your child's age!

MOM

CHILD: Draw the most beautiful flower bouquet!

CHILD

MOM: Add the most beautiful vase to put the flowers in!

MOM

CHILD: Draw your favorite season!

CHILD

MOM: Draw an activity you would like to do with your child in that season!

MOM

CHILD: Design a maze!

CHILD

MOM: Solve the maze!

MOM

CHILD: Draw an underwater world!

CHILD

MOM: Draw the sky above. How is the weather?

MOM

CHILD: Draw an alien!

CHILD

MOM: Draw the alien's mother!

MOM

CHILD: Draw your pet or the pet you would want!

CHILD

MOM: Add a pal for this pet! Draw them interacting in a silly or humorous way.

MOM

CHILD: Draw a castle for yourself!

CHILD

MOM: Draw the surrounding landscape.

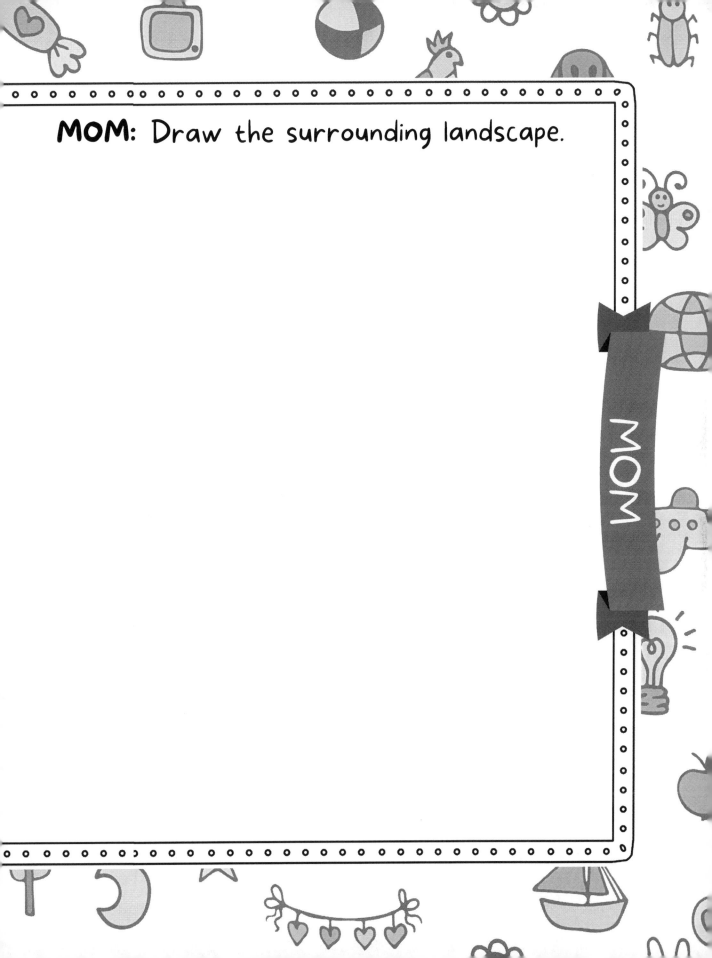

CHILD: Fill the page with butterflies!

CHILD

MOM: They are heading to an unexpected place. Draw it!

MOM

CHILD: Draw a happy Easter Bunny!

CHILD

MOM: Add an oversized Easter egg and decorate it!

MOM

CHILD: Draw a silly robot that will help you with some of your tasks.

CHILD

MOM: Draw one task he can accomplish!

CHILD: Draw a tree!

CHILD

MOM: Design a tree house!

MOM

Want FREEBIES?

Email Us At:

larasvows@gmail.com

Title the email "DRAW WITH MOM" and
let us know that you purchased our book.

_____

THANKS FOR YOUR AMAZING SUPPORT!

>>>>>>>>>>>>>>>>>>>>>>>>>>>>>>>

For Enquiries and Customer Service
email us at:

larasvows@gmail.com

We don't exist without you. A brief review could help us a lot. Please leave your feedback about this book.

SCAN THE OR CODE BELLOW

>>>>>>>>>>>>>>>>>>>>>>>>>>>>>>

THANKS FOR YOUR AMAZING SUPPORT!

Made in United States
Orlando, FL
15 December 2024

55734805R00061